LOOK TO HIM WHO IS ABLE
WHY ARE WE HERE?

Donna Williams

Copyright © Donna Williams

All rights reserved. No part of this publication may be produced, distributed, or transmitted in any form or by any means, including photocopying, recording, or other electronic or mechanical methods, without the prior written permision of the publisher, except in the case of brief quotations embodied in critical reviews and certain other noncommercial uses permitted by copyright law.

For permission requests, write to the publisher, addressed "Attention: Permissions Coordinator" at the email address below:

Life and Success Publishing

e-mail: info@lifeandsuccessmedia.com

www.lifeandsuccessmedia.com

Unless otherwise stated, all scripture quotations are taken from the Holy Bible, New King James Version. Quotations marked NKJV are taken from the HOLY BIBLE, NEW KING JAMES VERSION. Copyright © 1973, 1978, 1984 by International Bible Society. Used by permission of Hodder and Stoughton Ltd, a member of the Hodder Headline Plc Group. All rights reserved. "NKJV" is a registered trademark of International Bible Society.
UK trademark number 1448790.

Quotations marked KJV are from the Holy Bible,

King James Version.

ISBN Number: 978-1-907402-99-9

CONTENTS

1. Trust God.. 9
2. Life is a Roller Coaster with a plan 14
3. God's Plan for Us 31
4. Gods Grace – Testimonies 44
5. How can we fail with God's Promise. 51
6. How can you be alone? 55
7. Thanksgiving.. 59
8. Love 63
9. Praise 67
10. Warfare... 70
11 Restoration and Salvation 73

Acknowledgments

MAMA I DON'T WANT TO DIE! This was a statement made in a true movie I have watched. What a statement to make, why not make a statement like that you may ask yourself? Read on:

I have heard it time and time again. Someone says 'I don't want to die' or 'I am not ready to die yet', or 'why me', or 'God why are you doing this to me?'

Dear God we are so selfish, when we came into the World, we take on to ourselves all that the world has to offer! We make worldly goods so personal to us.

As we grow older, we take the understanding that one day we will die, that is a definite, it is the only guarantee we all have in life.

We see families and friends die around us all the time.

God did not lie to us about dying, He even sent his Son into the world to be born and to die. This is the best example we could ever require to understand the meaning of dying;

> **JOHN 3:16 FOR GOD SO LOVE THE WORLD THAT HE GAVE HIS ONLY BEGOTTEN SON, THAT WHOSOEVER BELIVETH IN HIM SHOULD HAVE ETERNAL LIFE.**

What an example, yet we still ask the question, 'why me?' Or 'I'm not ready yet', or 'God, why are you doing this to me?'

We all know that the only thing we all have in common is that we are all going to die.

ISAIAH 2:22 <u>Stop trusting in man, who has but a breath in his nostrils. Of what</u> account is he? Clearly tells us 'we are but breath in the nostrils; we will go like a blink of an eye and leave all our worldly positions behind.' When I read this verse, I ask myself,

"If we are following God's words and the teaching of Jesus, why can't we accept what is to come?" Thus, meaning that we all need to leave this Earth sooner or later.

As Christians, we all need to let go when God has said, therefore, when our expiry date is up, **it's up**!

Did you know we all come with an expiry date? The Bible tells us there is a time to laugh, a time to cry, a time to be born and a time to die. Read: **Ecclesiastes 3:2-8.**

I tell you now that it is not up to us whether we are ready or not. We all have a limited time on this Earth; A time of birth, and a time to die.

Some of us live longer than others, but only God knows the reason why we all have a different life span Therefore while we are on this Earth for a divine purpose, all God asks us to is that we live according to his word, by; Praising him, Worshiping Him and utilising our gift(s) by helping each other, especially those who are less fortunate than us. The sooner we accept this and do what God put us on the earth to do the better we will be when our time is cease up. Remember, while on Earth whatever we do in Jesus' name is not for our flesh, it is for our soul, a time after death.

It is simple. He wants us to live a clean life, to follow his instructions and do his will. But all we do is complain, if it rains we complain, if it snows, we complain, if it's sunny, we complain. If we have what we want financially we still complain that we haven't got enough money. Why? Because the more we have the more we spend and The more we see and the more we want. This is our human nature but if we are walking with God and in all his goodness we will change.

CHAPTER 1

Trust God

I am guilty of all the above, but I came from a journey, where I am so grateful for whatever little I have. Why? This is because I was not where I am now in my walk with God. **Jeremiah 29:11** tells me that God knows the plans he has for me (us), plans to prosper us and not to harm us, plans to give us hope and a future. Therefore I am trying to discipline my attitude towards spending. I am not there yet but I am getting there. We perish for lack of knowledge. So I implore you, get knowledgeable, read your Bible daily.

How amazing this is, to go about our business knowing that there is a promise that has been made over our life. A plan of prosperity, success and a plan to keep us from harm.

With promises' like this and others laid out for us (you me and the people) who has pass before us, including people in the Bible for example, all we need to do is have faith, believe and walk with your head high and know that God can turn any situation around for you.

When things go wrong we cast all blame to God and question him. Do you realise that God gave us authority, power and dominion over everything? (**Luke 10:19**) what kind of life are we living? Did you know you can use the power God has given you to change any situation or circumstances that occurs in your life?

You see, when Jesus died; **John 14:25 -26.** He said a comforter will come.

Now the Doctor may say to you, "you only have ex amount of time to live" Remember you are blessed, you have a weapon to change situations and circumstances, God can turn it around! I urge you that when you hear these words, do not let it take root. I know exactly what you are Thinking, 'it's ok for her to talk'. But I am talking from experience don't get me wrong "listen to the Doctors" it is all about having a balance and using wisdom.

God has given authority over all flesh to give eternal life to all who receive Jesus as their saviour. Eternal Life doesn't only mean when we die we will go to heaven, no. It also means that we all need to live God's life on earth. This is why John 17:3 it is written; 'be full with Christ on earth. 'All I am saying is you remember God's promise in your life.

Isaiah 2:22 says stop! Trusting in man! Who has but a breath in his Nostrils, what accounts is he? Think about it, only God can put a time on your life. Yes God gave man wisdom, knowledge and understanding. Therefore a Doctor can only speak from his medical experience, by anticipating a time.

NOTE: I am not telling you not to go to the Doctor, use wisdom; it is all about having a balance;

I will explain to you, why on many occasion people die on or round about the date the Doctor gave them. You see the minute the Doctor spoke those words over your life, you accepted them in your mind, and allowed it to plant into your body. Your body accepted it and roots started to form. Next thing you know your death has rived. What happened is that the person takes those words and planted it into their body. It is a mind over matter situation- like the Chicken and the Egg, the Chicken comes from the egg and the egg comes from the chicken.

I am here to tell you, if you know the God you serve and the power you have within you, you would go down on your knees and pray and fast over the situation. As a matter of fact you should be praying off those sicknesses from your life every day harp and relief would come to Saul!

Ask God to heal you, tell the enemy where to go and thank God for health and healing in your inner and outer parts. I urge you to do this daily. Do it when you are well, do it when you feel good, don't take anything for granted because, Satan, the Enemy is just sitting and waiting for an opportunity to get into your life. Like the three wise virgins keep oil in your lamp, keep the lamp burning, and be prepared!

Pray and Fast. Speak to God for he is your Deliverer, your Maker! He is the one who knows all things. He knows exactly when you should leave this Earth. He is the one who is qualified to put a time on your life. Only God holds your life line. Hallelujah! THANK GOD FOR JESUS! Thank God for loving us so.

I know I sound a bit hypercritical by saying do not question God when you have a serious illness for example cancer. But what am I saying here is, you have the sickness. Therefore use your energy and pray for salvation healing and restoration. Have faith and trust God and believe that you can overcome your illness and live. Do not let go, do not surrender don't let the enemy take you prematurely!

Note: what I am going to say now might sound a slightly contradicting but please try to understand. You see, even thou I mention Satan we cannot blame everything on him. Many of us, especially us Christians have a habit of blaming everything on Satan please! Don't get me wrong I am a child of God, Born again Sanctified, Holy Ghost Baptise there is no way I am on Satan side; What I am trying to say is that we are all humans, Christians and non Christians, sometimes our lifestyle can cause certain illnesses to come upon us. It comes from our neglect to our body, what we put into our body and not taking care of ourselves. I encourage you to start looking after yourself, don't give up, and trust in God! While, you trust him you are looking after your body. Your body is the temple of God; remember that Satan has no power over you; he only has power when we give it to him by being disobedient to God. **Luke 10:19** said we have been given power to stamp on the devil under our feet. He has no power at all. The sooner we can grab that the better we will be.

Corinthians 6:19-20 expresses that it is all about having that balance.

Your faith can give you a testimony to protest God's glory in your life for others to see and believe. Our body is a temple; it is a place for the Holy Spirit to dwell. Therefore we need to take care of it and cherish it.

Our body is loaned to us by God, so take care of it, don't abuse it and don't take life for granted. Remember we are new every morning. Offer up a prayer of thanksgiving to God every morning to acknowledge this.

CHAPTER 2

Life Is a Roller Coaster With A Plan

Life is a roller coaster; it runs both day and night. Some trips take place in the dark, where things are difficult to recognise and distinguish.

Isaiah 50:10 (NIV) Reads: "who among you that fears the Lord" that obeys the voice of his servant, which walks in darkness and has no light; let him trust in the name of the Lord and rely on his God." Yes! Folk, even the Christians and believers who says they fear God, and call on his name, Christians who obey the voice of the Lord will at times walk where there seems to be no light to guide their footsteps and no warmth to comfort there troubled mind, why? Because we are human and we let flesh takes over.

This is not a time of punishment, retribution, abandonment or rejection, no; these are times when God is working out the next important stage of your development. This is where he is applying you for greater works in his kingdom!

Remember, Jesus conquers Satan, he said you can kill me but I will come back because he stands on God's word. He stands on God's promise; He trust God; that same promise is given to us and remains the same today.

Therefore, I urge you; don't miss out on Gods purpose for your life. Circumstances will discourage you. Do not look at your circumstances, renew your mind and look at God's love for the world. God loves us so much that he sends his only son Jesus to be persecuted and die on the cross for our sake to save us from sin.

I remember my roller coaster ride; it was a very dark and lonely place to be, days were as bad as nights. At nights I couldn't sleep, nights seemed long and never ending. I remember praying and crying out to God, reminding him that I am his daughter and that he is my Father. I cried out and reminded God of his promise to me, I cried out for help times and times again, but noting was changing, until I read about people like David. 1st Samuel15:1-34 God gave Saul a specific instruction and he disobeyed him, therefore the Lord rejected Saul as King over Israel. I tell you there is a price to pay when you disobey God. In 1st Samuel 16:1-23 God sent Samuel to Jesse's (David's father) house because one of his sons was to be anointed. Samuel

16:6-7 explains that when Samuel arrived and saw Eliab he thought to himself, surely, the Lord's anointed stands here before the Lord but the Lord said to Samuel "**Do not consider his appearance or his height, for I have rejected him. The Lord does not look at the things man looks at. Man looks at the outward appearance, but)**

God looks at the heart. Samuel went to David's home, David's father Jesse sent his 7 sons one by one to be anointed but as they came to Samuel God told Samuel "no not that one" So Samuel asked David's father Jesse, Do you have any more sons?. Jesse replied yes my youngest son is attending to the sheep in the field. Samuel asked Jesse to send for his youngest son. When David arrived he was fine in appearance and handsome in features, then the Lord told Samuel to "Rise and anoint David because he is the one the Lord has chosen. Samuel took the horn of oil and anointed David in the presence of his brothers, from that day the Spirit of the Lord came upon David.

Can you see that what's yours is yours, what the Lord has for you is yours! Correct me if I am wrong but God chose David to be anointed and even thou his seven brothers were presented to Samuel they could not be anointed. Why, because it was not their calling the anointed was not theirs! Look at the one, who God chose, he was the one who was out in the field looking after the sheep. Therefore I urge you do what you are doing and serve in the Church. Don't watch what is going on with others, don't get jealous, be happy for them when they get their breakthrough. Congratulate them with a true and honest heart. Be happy for them, why, because your time will come!

I urge you to tell yourself that God is doing something for me, tell yourself everyday that God is working it may take some time but God is working. **Samuel 16:14-23** shows that after David was anointed the Spirit of the Lord left Saul and an evil spirit came upon him and tormented him. Saul asked one of his servants to find someone who plays the harp well and bring him to play when he is tormented with the evil spirit. Saul was told that Jesse had a son who plays the harp well. A messenger was sent to Jesse's home and asked if his son David would go to Saul. Jesse prepared a donkey loaded with bread, wine and a young goat and sent them with his young son David to Saul. In **1st Samuel 16:22-23** Saul sent words to Jesse asking if David could stay in his service for a while because he is pleased with him. Every time the evil spirit came upon Saul, David would play the harp and relief would come to Saul

David Killed Goliath.

In **1st Samuel 17**: there was a war between the Israelites and the Philistines; the city was divided between the two. The Philistines occupied one hill and the Israelites another and the valley between them. A champion named Goliath from Garth came out of the Philistine camp. He was nine feet tall, he had a Bronx helmet on his head and wore a coat of scales, armour of bronze weighing five thousand shekels, on his legs he wore bronze greaves and a bronze javelin slung on his back. In **1st Samuel 17: 8** Goliath stood and cried out to the Armies of Israel, and said unto them, am I not a Philistine and you a servant of Saul? "Choose from your army and let him come against me" if he is able to fight me and kill me, we will be your servant but if I kill him then you will be our servant. When Saul and the armies of Israel heard the words of Goliath they became frightened and terrified. When David heard the words of Goliath, he investigated of the armies saying! What will happen to the man who kills the Philistine? When his brother Eliab heard David speaking to the men of the army he became angry and said to David why have you come here? Who have you left the few sheep in the wilderness with the wild animals? I know your pride and the wickedness of your heart; because you have come down to see the battle. David turned away from his brother and asked the question again from another man, what will happen to the man who kills the Philistine? David was told that the man who kills Goliath the king will give his daughter and make his father's house free in Israel. Now the men of the Army went to Saul and told him that David is enquiring about killing Goliath, Saul sent and called David. 1st **Samuel 17:32** David told Saul let no man's heart fail because of him; thy servant will go and fight the Philistine. In verse 34 Saul said to David; you can't fight Goliath you are only a youth and he has been a fighter since he was a youth. David staid to Saul in the same verse 34, when I was looking after my father's sheep and a lion and a bear took a lamb from the flock I would go after it and smote (Strike) it and take the lamb from it's mouth, and when he would come against me I would hold it by the beard and strike it and slew it. Thy servant Slew both lion and bear therefore this un-circumcised Philistine who comes up against the armies of the living God is noting for me to kill. Moreover David said 'the Lord that delivered me out of the paw of the Lion and the paw of the bear will deliver me out of the hand of the Philistine'. Saul said to David; to go and the Lord be with you. The Lord delivers David out of the hand of Goliath.

Saul gave David armours to wear and David put them aside and said he has never worn them before therefore he didn't need them and he took them off. David chose five stones and with his staff in his hand he put the stones into his shepherd's bag and his sling in his hand, then he drew near to Goliath.

Life Is a Roller Coaster With A Plan

Watch this, Goliath came and drew near to David and when he saw David, Goliath said to David you are but a youth, am I a dog that you come to me with staves? Then Goliath cursed David's God then he said to David; come to me I will kill you and feed your flesh to the bird of the air and to the beast of the fields.

Read what happens!

> **David said to Goliath you come to me with sword and a spear and shield BUT I CAME TO YOU IN THE NAME OF THE LORD OF HOSTS THE GOD OF THE ARMIES OF ISRAEL, WHOM THOU HAS DEFIED. THIS DAY THE LORD WILL DELIVER YOU INTO MY HAND AND I WILL SMITE YOU AND TAKE YOUR HEAD FROM YOU; AND I WILL GIVE THE CARCASES OF THE OHOS OF THE PHILISTINES THIS DAY UNTO THE BIRDS OF THE AIR AND TO THE WILD BEAST OF THE EARTH MAY KNOW THAT THERE IS A GOD OF ISRAEL, AND ALL WILL KNOW THAT THE LORD SAVETH NOT WITH SWORD AND SPEAR, FOR THE BATTLE IS THE LORD'S AND HE WILL GIVE YOU INTO OUR HANDS.**

Next day David rose up early and ran towards the army where he ran towards Goliath, David put his hand in his bag, and took a stone and slangs it and smote Goliath in his forehead, the stone sank into Goliath's forehead and he fell upon his face to the ground. David ran unto Goliath and took Goliath's sword, kills him and then he beheaded him. When the Philistine saw what had happened they ran with fear

and the army of the Israelites shouted with Joy and ran after the Philistines who fell down by the wayside and the Israeli Army returned from chasing after them.

The moral of the story is; God was with David from the beginning. Read 1st Samuel 18-30 and see for yourself how after David Killed Goliath Saul became jealous of David and chased him to kill him. You would also see how God delivered Saul into David's hand and David did not kill him even when he had the opportunity. Following on, read how Saul's son Jonathan became a good friend of David and told David to hide in the cave to save him from the wrath of his father. Also, read how even when David was hiding in the cave God was with him and didn't leave him. Finally read the 2nd book of Samuel and see how he escaped Saul and eventually became one of the greatest Kings in Israel.

Can you see where I am coming from; God has the last word in all our lives, not the Doctors, not the Devil, not circumstances or People. Stay on the Roller coaster ride and trust God; he is planning your future like he planned David's, life after your life and many others.

I came through my roller coaster ride with a Job that suits my purpose. That's what God is about.

Think of Moses, think of his life, His Roller Coaster Ride. I'll take you through Mosses' life; read the book of Exodus and see the reason God brought Moses into the world. It was no accident Moses came into the world when he did. Moses parents were Levites; Levites worship the true and living God.

Pharaoh and his people worship idle.

After Moses' mother gave birth to him she hid him for three months.

When she couldn't hide him anymore, she made a basket, sealed it with tar and put The baby in it and put it on the river banks amongst the bushes.

Moses' sister was left hiding in the bush to see who would pick up the basket with the child. The plan was that his mother wanted to know what would happen to her son. Pharaohs' Daughter went to bathe in the river Nile with one of her attendants. She went walking along the river bank, and saw the basket amongst the bushes. She called her attendants to go and fetch the basket and was surprised to see a baby in it. When Pharaoh's daughter looked at the child she knew straight away the child was one of the Hebrew babies. She took the child home as her son.

Moses Mother and Sister work at the Palace, so Moses' sister asked Pharaoh's daughter if she should go and get one of the Hebrew women to nurse the child and Pharaoh's daughter said yes.

Can you see God's plan?

Moses sister went and got her mother; in return Moses' own mother nursed him in the Palace but he grew up with the knowledge that he was the son of Pharaoh's daughter.

This is where you can see God's plan for Moses' life. God knew that one day Moses would go back to the Palace of his childhood to speak to Pharaoh. Therefore Moses grew up in the Palace, as Pharaoh's own son and Prince of Egypt.

One Day Moses went out to where the Hebrew people were hard at work in the place where they were held as slaves by Pharaoh. Moses saw an Egyptian being beaten by an Egyptian man. Remember Moses did not know he was a Hebrew. Seeing the man being beaten, Moses glanced around to make sure no one else was in sight and he killed the Egyptian and hid him in the sand.

Now as you read on, remember it is importance to be careful of your actions.

The next day Moses saw two Hebrews fighting, when he went up to the men and asked the one in the wrong, why are you hitting your brother? The Hebrew answered, who are you to judge? Are you going to kill me like you killed the Egyptian? Therefore Moses became afraid and ran away.

God's plan for Moses' life started to form. This is where God prepared Moses for his journey to lead the people out of Egypt. Moses is now in training but he just doesn't know it. After Moses ran away he spent many days and nights wandering in the desert with nowhere to go, until he came to a well where he met his wife. **They married, had children, there he stayed with his wife, their children and his father in law; until God told him to go to Egypt and tell Pharaoh to let God's**

people go. This is where experience and training came in handy; I'm breaking this down now. After many miracles Pharaoh eventually let the people go. Moses and the Hebrew people walked around the Desert for forty days and forty nights sometimes hungry and thirsty. Let me round this up for you. I call this a set up, God set up Moses to be born to a Hebrew woman who worked in Pharaoh's Palace. The Hebrews was slaves to Pharaoh. At the time of Moses' birth Pharaoh made a law to kill all Hebrew first born, including their cattle.

Moses' mother like any other mother did not want her child to be killed. That is why she came up with the idea to hide her child amongst the bushes. When she couldn't hide him any longer she put him in the basket on the river Nile.

Now Let's look at the way God works; another part of the plan was for Moses to grow up in the palace as a Prince, so that when he goes to the Palace to speak to Pharaoh about freeing the Hebrews, Nothing in the Palace would take his focus from what he went there to do.

Why? This is because he grew up there therefore he was on **familiar ground**.

Now remember when Moses killed the Egyptian? He ran away and wandered around in the desert on his own not knowing where he was going another plan of God's.

What Moses didn't know was he was on a training course. Stay with me, I am wrapping this up.

Now when the Hebrews', God's people were in the desert they complained and complained to Moses. They even blamed him for taking them out of Egypt, some said They would rather have stayed with Pharaoh as slave because at least they would have had food. With Moses' previous experience in the desert he was able to tell them to push through and don't go back.

You see Moses ran the course before, God prepared Moses to do the job therefore it must be completed. Think of an athlete before they run a big race. They practice on the track first so they know and feel what it is like. Therefore nothing would come as a surprise to them when the big race comes. There are no distractions and no surprises.

(Note well) If you live with a blind person and you know that person knows where the door is in the house, you are not going to move that door are you?

I keep saying to people**, Look to Him Who Is Able.** Read your Bible, Believe, Stand on his word, know God for yourself, and believe in yourself. Trust God. There is no rocket science with the bible and knowing God. All you need is to have a balance.

Please note: If you don't understand what you read, ask God for wisdom, clarification and understanding. Also read the book of Proverbs to gain wisdom.

It takes preparation and process. **Believe, have faith, Stand on God's word and most important fast,** as you go along you will find that everything falls into place like a jig saw puzzle. Your relationship with God is also based on your lifestyle. You will get to understand this more when you have a personal relationship with God.

I remember a poem I wrote titled 'My relationship with Christ', I remember explaining how I feel having a relationship with my Heavenly Father. It's like waking up in Jamaica at 4am sitting on the Veranda, everything is still and quiet, a calm feeling in the atmosphere, everything and everyone is still and warm, no one is awake. I remember thinking when I was sitting there that morning, how peaceful and quiet this is, what a wonderful experience; this is how my relationship with Christ is.

This thought brings me to a young man I worked with some years ago. He had no peace in his marriage, why because he is a Muslim, Indian origin the young man in question confirmed to me that he believed in God, he said he read his Bible everyday and prayed all the time.

Sitting opposite this young man at work every day, one day he confided in me about his feelings and told me about the verbal abuse he gets from his wife and her family, because during his four years of marriage his wife has not got pregnant.

You see being Muslim he had an arranged marriage therefore his marriage needed to be blessed with an offspring. (A Child) but this wasn't happening.

He was anxious, depressed, and very unhappy and often blamed himself. He said his wife called him 'useless' and on many occasions she would go off on holiday with her family and leave him at home alone. The young man and his wife paid out lots of Money by going to various fertile clinics and various private doctors getting treatments after treatments to have a child.

He became withdrawn, shameful and felt useless as a man.

I told him to keep trusting and believing in God that his wife will get pregnant.

I also told him to stop spending all that money on doctors, slow down, pray, believe and trust God and it will happen.

I explained to him that God can change any situation and anything; I told him that God is able. I explained to him that he should stop focusing on the problem so much because it is giving him anxiety and stress and it's making the situation worse.

I told him that his wife will get pregnant but it will be all in God's timing and not his timing and certainly not in his wife and her family's timing.

I told him that if he keeps focusing on the situation so much he is only forcing the problem prematurely, and if God is not involved it would be no good, it will be spoilt.

So he stopped going to the Doctors, I continued to pray with him, and over his situation.

He himself started to focus on God more and more. He became more relaxed and less and less stressed. I advised him to start going out with his wife more and enjoy each other which he did. I left the Job but kept in touch with him and continued to pray with him. I prayed with him many times and never stop praying. I believe in the saying Push until something happens.

Eight months later his wife became pregnant, and gave birth to not one child but two; twin girls. When I heard the news I offered up a praise of thanks giving to God, and gave God all the Glory.

Jeremiah 29:11. I said to him, to look to him who is able, your maker and creator who knows the plan he has for you, plans for you to be successful and prosper and not plans to kill you or bring you down.

When you know, that you know the God you serve and the love he has for you, you can do all things through Jesus Christ.

Father, Forgive us for we know not what we do or say.

Proverbs 3:5-10 Trust in the Lord with all your heart and lean not on your own understanding. In all your ways acknolowledge him, and he will make your path straight. Do not be wise in your own eyes, fear the lord and put evil out of your life.

In doing that, it will bring health to your body and nourishment to your bones.

Honour the lord with your wealth and first fruits of your crops. Pay your tides and offerings and give God your thanks and praise for what he has provided and for what he has done in your life, this includes health and provision from sickness and he will give you everything you want without limits.

Proverbs 16:3 says commit to the Lord whatever you do and your plan will succeed.

Note Well: It is amazing the conversation that goes on while travelling on public transport.

I remember travelling on the bus to work one morning, when I overheard a conversation between a young girl and her mother. This young lady was talking on her mobile phone to her mother. The young lady in question look stoned drunk or totally stoned on drugs. Her fingers were orangey yellow, I remember thinking is she ill or what? Her words to her mother were; 'I have to go back to hospital; they are going to keep me in one more week'. From the conversation her mother was elderly and was asking questions about her smoking habit, the young lady said to her mother "I am now down to 40 a day. I use to smoke 60 a day! I am better with the smoking now she said. Then the words that followed made me sit there and start asking God to forgive her. I remember saying over and over, Father forgive us for we know not what we say. This young lady said to her mother, **'oh sod it I may as well die. It's not worth it, my life is shitty anyway, if, I die I die'.** I remember thinking to myself how sad the way we abuse our body which the Lord has entrusted us with. How sad to blame everyone else for our mess and then we use words like it's my life, it's my body. All I found myself saying again is Father; forgive us, for we know not what we say. I can't even imagine what her life must be like for her to be telling her elderly mother" I may as well die"

Thinking about it now, I should have gone to that young lady and told her about Jesus. I should have told her how he loves her, I should have told her he can change her and make her well, I should have told her it didn't need to be that way, I should have told her about the precious gift of life God has given her, I should have told her that if she wants, she can turn her life around for the better. I should have told her that she didn't even need to go back into that hospital, all she had to do was pray, ask Jesus into her life, I should have told her he is only a prayer away and he is waiting for her invite. All she needs to do was to just call his name and change would come But, I didn't why? It's because I wasn't where I am now in my walk in Christ.

I remember another conversation on the bus with an elderly lady complaining to her friend about all the aches and pains she had, she was naming and complaining. I remember thinking to myself; stop talking to others who cannot help you. To me that was wasted energy. I remember saying to myself; take it to the Lord in prayer, take it to the creator, your maker, and take it to the one who can help.

I know they say a problem shared is a problem halved. I remember thinking to myself take it to God in prayer, friend cannot help you. If only we can grasp the words of God use the tools he has given us put it into action, for example **Matthew 18:20** for where two or three come together in my name. Rather than complaining if we get together and say lets pray for change, lets pray for the pain to go, lets pray for the that person who is sick in bed or in the hospital. Let's do less complaining and more praying together.

Another thing I remember observing while travelling on the bus was a young man standing at a bus stop holding a crutch, one of his leg was bandaged, he had the crutch under his arm, the bandage foot slightly lifted off the ground, he has a can of beer in his and a lit cigarette in the other hand. I watched him took a drink from the beer then a puff from the cigarette.

He repeated the process continually, again all I did was say Father God help him, send an angel to minister to him and show him who you are and tell him how much you love him. So many of us are trapped in this corrupted world and not knowing you for who you are. "A mighty God "A God who can move us from society within a split second, **Matthew 14 17:21** A God that made the mountains move. A God of everlasting power.

O how I fear God, when I think of his power and might. I am not the sea, I am not the mountains, I am a person walking around on this earth for a short period of time, my time was bought with a price, my life has already been paid for, my sins have already been forgiven. My entire being was not cheap, it cost a great price and it cost the life of a great King, the greatest King everlasting, a King who died and spilled his blood and rose from the dead for you and me! To give us new life and a new beginning! To give us freedom from slavery of sin, to give us success, to give us power to conquer everything in our father's name, to give us restoration.

2nd Chronicles 7:14 reads: God says '*if my people who are called by my name will humble themselves and pray and seek my face, and turn from their wicked ways, then I will forgive their sins and will heal their land*'. This is God's promise, not man's broken promises, God's promise and words stand forever; yesterday, today and forever.

How awesome it is that my life has already been mopped out. The formula has been done, ready and waiting for fulfilment. It is waiting to explode. The water is troubled waiting for us to step out in faith.

Chapter 3.
God's Plan for Us

As I was writing this book I found myself thinking of the plans God has for us.

Sometimes we found ourselves in places or situations we never dreamt we would be in. Sometimes the situation are not to our standard, sometimes they are unpleasant but when we are in these places we think to ourselves why me? Sometimes it is not totally our fault why certain thing happened to us. I have news for you, guess what? Some of the things we go through or some situations and places we found ourselves in we don't know it yet but it's all part of **God's Plan. It is a test, it is a ride we are on, to get through to the other side for our victory, and give birth to something that God has planned for us.**

Here are 9 points to remember about going through the storms in your life.

1. Go through the storm; remember God is there with you.
2. Remember it is all part of God's Plan

3. Don't give up, no one said it would be easy

4. Think positive, the road will be rough but go through the storm, ride the wave.

5. Remember that you are on a training course

6. Remember God's word, stay on the course, he will bring you through it and he will never leave you.

7. Think of the victory at the end.

8. Know that you will never be the same again, your growth when you come through the storm and out of your unpleasant situation, will make you a better person.

9. **Look to him who is able**, you are the head and not the tail.

And most important of all Remember God when you get your victory, Give him the glory. This is very, very important!

Two people stood out in my mind most. These people found themselves in unpleasant situations; one is Joseph Genesis 37-50. I will break the story down and make it understanding and as clear as possible.

Joseph a seventeen year old young man, this young man lives with his father and brothers. Joseph looks after his father's flocks; Joseph was his father's favourite son because he was the youngest. Joseph was born to his father when his father was old in age. Joseph's father loves him so much that he made him a multi-colour coat. His brothers hated him because of the love their father had for him and the way he treated him.

One night Joseph has a dream, and when he told it to his brothers they hated him even more. Joseph explained his dream to his brothers. Genesis 37-6:-11. Joseph said to his brothers, 'listen to this dream, we were binding the sheaves of corn out in the field when suddenly my sheaves rose and stood upright, while yours sheaves gathered round mines and bowed down to it'. His brothers said 'do you intend to reign over us?' They hated him even more because of his dream and what he said.

Then he had another dream and told them, saying to his brothers 'I had another dream, this time the sun and moon and eleven stars were bowing down to me'.

When he told his brothers and his father the second dream, his father rebuked him Saying, 'what is this dream you had? Will your mother and I and your brothers actually come and bow down to the ground before you?' His brothers were jealous of him but his father kept the matter in mind.

One day Joseph's brothers were out in the field minding the flocks, Joseph's father called him and send him out to see if all is well with his brothers. Joseph was to return to his father and report to him if all is well with his brothers.

When Joseph arrived in the fields a man saw him wondering around and asked him what he was looking for? My brothers he replied, can you tell me where they are?

They have moved on from here answered the man "I heard them say they are going to Dothan" therefore, Joseph went off to Dothan in search of his brothers,

His brothers saw him in the distance and said to each other.

'Here comes the dreamer come let's kill him and throw him into the one of these castanets! And say that a vicious animal devoured him then we will see what comes of his dreams'.

When his brother Reuben heard this he tried to rescue him by saying, "let's not take his life, and don't shed his blood. Throw him into the cistern here in the desert, but don't lay hands on him".

Reuben's plan was to rescue his brother Joseph from them and take him back to their father. But when Joseph came near his brothers, they stripped off his robe his father made and throw him into the cistern.

The cistern was empty with no water in it, as they were eating the meal they saw a caravan of Ishmaelite coming from Gilead, their camels were loaded with spices, balm, and myrrh, they were on their way to Egypt. Judah said to his brothers, lets sell him to the Ishmaelite after all, he is our brother, our own blood and flesh and they all agreed.

So when the indianite merchants came by they pulled their brother Joseph out of the cistern and sold him for twenty shekels of silver to the Ishmaelite who took him to Egypt. **Watch this**!

This is the beginning of a Journey in Joseph's life where he found himself in a strange place away from his family and the love of his father; this is how God is setting him up for future plans to be accomplished.

Sometimes God will even take you away from the love of your family and put you in unfamiliar places to fulfil his plans and purpose. You will understand what I mean when I carry on this story;

God's Plan for Us

Joseph was sold by his brothers and was taken to Egypt.

When Rueben his brother return to the cistern he saw that Joseph was not there. He went back to his father and told him that Joseph was not there, meanwhile his brothers killed a goat and dipped Joseph's Robe in the blood and took it to

His father, and said they found it, they told their father that it looks like Joseph has been killed by a wild animal.

Their father recognized the robe as Joseph's Robe. Jacob, their father tore off his robe (his clothes) and put on sack cloth and mourned for Joseph his son many days. All his sons and daughters came to Jacob but he refused them, he wanted to die with his son Joseph so he wept and wept for many days. Meanwhile the Ishmaelite sold Joseph in Egypt to Potiphar, one of Pharaoh's official, the captain of the guard.

Now the Lord was with Joseph and Joseph lived in Potiphar's house. Joseph gained favour in the eyes of Potiphar and with the Lord with him, everything he did he was successful. So Potiphar put him in charge of his household and he trusted Joseph with everything he owned. The Lord blessed the household of the Egyptian, because of Joseph the blessings of the Lord was on everything that potiphar owned or had in the household and in the field therefore he left Joseph in charge of everything he had. With Joseph taking care of all potiphar's possessions'

The only care Potiphar had was the food he was eating.

Joseph became successful in everything he did.

Joseph was well built and handsome and Potiphar's wife started to notice him and invited him to go to bed with her. Joseph refused and told her "my master does not concern himself with anything in this house, he trusts me with everything including you" Why should I do such a wicked thing and sin against God? My master has withheld nothing from me but you! (**THE PLOT**)

Every day Potiphar's wife asked Joseph to go to bed with her and Joseph refused, Joseph even refused to go to be alone with her. One day Joseph went into the house to attend to his duties. There was one of the household servants in the house and Potiphar's wife grab hold of Joseph's cloak, Joseph pulled away and left his cloak in her hand and ran out of the house. When she saw Joseph ran away and leave his cloak in her hand she called her maidservant and told him, "Look Joseph came in here to sleep with me and I screamed and he ran away leaving his cloak".

When his master came home she told him what Joseph did and his master was very angry and put Joseph prison. But God was with Joseph Why? Joseph was innocent and was shown favour by the prison warden.

The warden put Joseph in charge of all those in prison and made him responsible for all that was done there. Again Joseph became successful in everything he did and the warden paid attention to All Things under Joseph care.

Watch how God start to work to get Joseph's release from prison.

Genesis 40 – Some-time later the Cup bearer and the baker of the King of Egypt offended their master the King of Egypt. He was angry with them and put them both into custody in the house of the captain of the guard, the same prison of which Joseph was in charge. After they have been in prison for some time the baker and the cupbearer had a dream which had no meaning to them. When Joseph came to them in the morning he saw that they were troubled, so he asked them 'why are your faces so sad today?'

'We both had a dream' they said, but there is no one to interpret them.

Joseph said, 'do not interpretations belong to God? Tell me your dreams' Josephs said. So they both told Joseph their dreams and Joseph interprets the dreams telling them that within three days Pharaoh will restore them back to their rightful place in the palace. **Genesis 40:6-14 Joseph told the cupbearer that when he has been re-instated, to help get him out of prison.** When the baker saw that Joseph had a gift to interpret dreams, he told Joseph his dream **Genesis 40:16-23**

The third day came when the dream Joseph interpreted came to pass and the baker lost his head and the cupbearer was reinstated but after all that, the cupbearer did not remember Joseph. In fact he forgot him.

Genesis 41 Two years pass, then, Pharaoh had a dream and it troubled his mind but none of his own men could interpret his dream. Then the cup bearer said to Pharaoh, I remember when you were upset with me and confined me to prison. I

and the baker had a dream and a man by the name of Joseph interpreted our dreams and everything he said came to pass.

Stay with me I am getting there, rounding this up now. So Pharaoh sent for Joseph, after Joseph washed, shaved and changed his clothes, he came before Pharaoh.

Genesis 41:14 Pharaoh told Joseph his dream so Joseph told Pharaoh about the seven good years and seven bad years of famine to follow.

So Pharaoh put Joseph in charge of the whole land of Egypt.

Imagine God's plan coming to pass; now Joseph is in charge of all the Land of Egypt. When famine spread over the whole Land of Egypt, Joseph opened the storehouse and sold grain to all the Egyptians because the famine was severe in the land of Egypt and the entire world.

Now Watch This- Joseph brothers went to Egypt to buy grain.

I will break down the rest of the story now; Joseph brothers went to buy grain, when Joseph saw them he reconsidered them as his brothers and returned the money by hiding it in the middle of the sack of grain. Talk about keeping a cool head.

This is what happens when God is with you. They went home and couldn't understand why the money was given back to them. Their father sent them back with the money to buy more grain and Joseph revealed himself to his brothers.

Genesis 42 43-45 and they went and brought their father Jacob to Egypt to meet his beloved son Joseph.

Joseph introduced the entire family to Pharaoh and the family remained in Egypt for some years.

I promise you God has a plan for each and every one of us. It doesn't matter where we go or where we have been. I encourage you to stay on the course. Keep your eyes on the prise (God) and see the end result.

Now for a modern Day Joseph: Unfortunately He Pass Away before I Publish This Book.

Another plan God had for a very important man which is still alive to this day. Nelson Mandela, a South Africa Anti-Apartheid Leader-turn President.

We all know the story, all I am asking you to do, is to read between the lines and see the plan God had for his life, then look at your life and consider making a change in your life also. No, it doesn't have to be as drastic as all the people I wrote about e.g. going into to prison, look at your life and see where you are going there is a plan for all of us.

I remember as a teenager round about the age of 17, I use to wear a badge**, which says. "FREE NELSON MANDELLA"**. Looking back now, if someone asked Me back then, why I am wearing the badge, I don't think I could say much, only that it said Free Nelson Mandela? I guess I didn't fully understood exactly what the words on the badge stood for. I only knew that everyone I associated with at that time was wearing the badge and big afro hair style. Everywhere I went people were talking about Nelson Mandela, my parents, friends, brothers and people in the streets. Even my baby brother age 9 would shout out, "Free Nelson Mandela"

Wow! I didn't know I was a follower, me, little skinny 6 stones 17 years old who thought she was the best thing going. I thought back then I had a mind of my own. Nelson Mandela was a young man about age 25 to 26 with lots of followers fighting against apartheid. (Meaning the division in his country of birth, South Africa). Nelson and his followers fought against division amongst the people in his country. Blacks cannot do this, Blacks cannot do that, Blacks cannot go there etc. But because of Nelson Mandela's empowerment (rephrase; spirit of rebellion is) knowing that God made us all equal, he challenged and fought back but he was caught and put into prison for 27 years.

The Opposition didn't know it, that by putting him in prison they were making Mandela more powerful and stronger.

God's plan for his life had started. Nelson Mandela came out of prison in 1990 age 72 and became Prime Minister of South Africa over Blacks and Whites. One Sunday during his Presidentship he interrupted an ANC black riot – South Africa supporters meeting – Mandela asked them to throw away their Guns and Knives into the sea. He then explained to the people that there is a better way to have peace and equality than fighting with knives and guns. He told them that he believe in forgiveness, and liberation. Mandela told them that the rainbow starts here.

What he explained to them is that it's time for Black people and White people to start relating." He went on to explain to them that he spent 27 years in prison reading their books and studying them, learning about them. Surprise them with compassion, generosity and kindness, and by doing this it will help to renew their nation.

They all did exactly what Mandela said meanwhile Mandela learnt all about the biggest Rugby team in Africa called the spring ball. He memorized the player's name, one day just before the game starts, while they were on the field Nelson made a surprise visit when, he went and shook all the players hand and call them by name and wish them good luck. They were so surprised, and asked each other 'is this man for real, firstly fighting against us and secondly he visited us as though we are his friend'. **CAN YOU SEE GOD WORKING HERE? SURPRISE YOUR ENEMIES WITH KINDNESS! WOW** I hope you can see what I can see.

They asked themselves, 'Is this the same man we put in jail?' After that incident Mandela called the captain of the rugby team and invited him to have tea at his home.

The Captain started to talk to the rest of the team saying to them that Mandela is an old man with a heart of gold and that they need to give him a chance, because he wants to unite blacks and whites and he wants peace in the country. The captain of the rugby team arranged for the rugby team to visit the prison cell, where, Mandela spent 30 years of his time while in prison.

Cell 646 - 1964. On the wall of the prison cell they noticed an inscription written by Mandela. Quoted Prisoner 646, 1994 'I am the Master of my faith and the captain of my soul'.

Success is within all of us. You can change any situation you are in, Trust God, Believe in him, believe in yourself and success will take place. How refreshing is that inscription to the human race?

After that visit, to the cell, the rugby team decided to sing a song which they originally refused to sing at the opening ceremony of a very important game.

The song is called God Bless Africa. The entire country was overjoyed and celebrated the team. That day they were hugging each other, Black people hugging White people. Amazing unity and peace began from that day onwards, and still remain so to this day.

There is no secret what God can do! If he can do it for Mandela he can do it for you. The same rule applies to all of us; with God there is no favouritism. We are all equal in the sight of God.

The same covenant he made with Abraham is the same covenant he made with all mankind, remember his word stands forever, it never changes.

Let me make this clear for you, **Jeremiah 29:11;** 'for I know the plan I have for you', declares the Lord, 'Plans for wholeness and not for evil, to give you a future and a hope'. I can't elaborate on this verse anymore, eat it, swallow it and digest it, bury it deep into your soul and start to see thing happened in your life for the better. You see God knows the plan he has for each and everyone of us, sometimes the road is dark and rocky, sometimes we don't understand why we are going through certain situations, sometimes we asked the question why me? Sometimes we curse God; O' yes many people curse God"

Many people asked the question;' God why is this happening to me? Some says 'I don't understand', some said 'I can't take this anymore' and the real scary one is "I am going to end it all!" Some do end it all by taking their life, some try but don't succeed. All we need to do is have patience, sit tight, go through the storm and wait on God to see the outcome. I know what you are thinking easier said than done. Remember! **Jeremiah 29:11 and go through the storm, Because just at that time when you want to quit or end it, that is when you are about to get your breakthrough. But, because you quit guess What you miss it. Wow! Just wait a little longer, asks God to give you that spirit of patience.**

CHAPTER 4
Gods Grace –Testimonies

On October 2010 I received a text on my phone: text read 'please pray for my seven year old Niece, in Hospital, she has just been diagnosed with a rear form of Leukaemia (Cancer of the Blood). The Doctors said she has a virus and may not survive'.

I had no idea who sent the text because there was no name. I wondered to myself, who send the text and whose niece is this? I came to the conclusion that it doesn't matter who send the text, it is irrelevant, and all I need to do is pray so I started to pray.

My prayers were, 'Father you know who is the sender who took the time to send me this text asking for prayer for his or her niece. I pray healing over this child's life Lord Jesus; I declare that by the stripes on your back she will be healed, by the power invested in me I cover her with a blanket of your blood Lord Jesus from the top of her head to the sole of her feet, in her inner parts and her outer parts. Lord Jesus I pray healing over this beautiful angel, who has been infected with this disease. Thank you for her life Lord, thank you for healing. Lord Jesus I praise you and give you thanks'.

This was my prayer every day over this child's life. One Day in March, I decided to phone a friend whom I haven't heard from for a while. She answered the phone, "Thank you for your prayer for my niece" she is still in hospital but two weeks ago the doctors did a complete test on her and there is no sign of Leukaemia.

All I could say was Praise God for his faithfulness and his words. Thank God for healing she and I pray for his continue healing over her life.

You see folks, how good is Our God? He sees and knows all things!

My Niece, who lives in Australia, is now six years old, when she was four years old she caught a disease from playing with a cat. Within minutes of being scratched by the cat, she developed a high temperature and her body was covered with a rash. She was rushed into hospital and placed into intensive care. She was unconscious **I urge you to look to no one but God. I urge you to look to him who is able**.

My brother and his wife were told that the disease she caught from the cat kills most children and only a small percentage survive. They told my brother that my niece only had a 10% chance of survival. When my brother told me this, I told him that I will call every member of the family I can get hold of and arrange for us all to pray for healing over my niece for 7 days (at night only, at 7pm. Why at night only you may ask, because everyone would be home from work and we would pray in our own home at the same time without any disruption.

For seven nights we prayed at 7pm. I would ring everyone to check if they prayed the answer was always yes. On the eighth day my brother phoned to say my niece was awake, smiling at her parents, she ate and the rashes have started to,

Disappear. All I could say was 'Praise God, to God be the glory **I urge you to look to no one but God. I urge you to look to him who is able**'. My Niece got better and is now six years old. Praise God. There is nothing God cannot do. (Jeremiah **I urge you to look to no one but God. I urge you to look to him who is able I urge you to look to no one but God. I urge you to look to him who is able**)

God is my healer; in 1990 I had an emergency operation, in my right eye. I was told I had Glaucoma in both eyes and lost ¾ of the sight in my right eye, I was told that the operation was necessary to save me from going blind totally in the right eye because the Glaucoma was developing rapidly. I was told that I would need to put drops into both eyes for the rest of my life. I was on four bottles of Drops which was installed into my eyes twice a day. At times my eyes hurt so badly at the sight of any light, daylight, lights on in the home, lights from oncoming cars. I had big problems. Sometimes my head is wrapped with a black

Cloth while being taken to the hospital. The hospital would put me in a dark room without any sign of light. Many times in Church my eyes hurt from watching a film or the light in the church.

For those of you who don't know what Glaucoma is, it is high blood pressure in the eye, I have been told that it links to a person who has diabetes; strangely enough I don't have diabetes.

On many occasions when I went to the hospital with pain in my eyes, the medical team said the pain is called eyeritis, this happened when the pressure is up in the eye and causes infection in the eye.

The pain was unbelievable, it starts from the front of the eye and goes through the middle right through to the back of the eye and a headache develops instantly.

In July 2010 I went to Israel with my Bishop and seven people from my church. I decided to get baptised in the river Jordan, as I stood in the water in the Jordan river my prayer to God was to heal me from all my health problems including healing for my eyes. That same night I stopped taking the eye drops, believing that I was healed, by the third day my eyes became blood red, and the pain started to surface. I decided to take the drops and wait on God. After that I started to pray for healing over my eyes, I would say to God, you are a God of light therefore as your child I need to be in the light, not a dark room at the hospital. I use to say to God 'How can the Holy Spirit live within me, whilst my eyes cannot look at the light? The devil is a liar'.

I continued to take the drops until just over a year later. August 2010, one lunch time at work I started to search the whole building for my glasses.

I had many of my colleagues looking for my glasses and couldn't find it. Someone at work lend me one of those pairs you buy in the pound shop or the chemist. Don't get me wrong, there was nothing wrong with them **I urge you to look to no one but God. I urge you to look to him who is able**. I worked perfectly well with them all afternoon.

That night when I went home, I found that the glasses were in my hand bag all the time. Three days later action replay, the same thing happened, I couldn't find my glasses. That was when I realised that I read my Bible with small prints on the train that morning, I read the newspaper on the train without my glasses, and at work I used the computer without my glasses. I suddenly realised that I didn't need the glasses as often as before. I am still trusting in God for total healing in my eyes. I am not where I ought to be yet but I am getting there. To God be the Glory, I know he will come through for me. My eyes will be totally healed.

Did you know that God sends healing Angels to heal us? Read on.

One morning in April 2007 I was lying in bed with two swollen feet, I couldn't walk. My feet were probing, my head hurt and I was feeling sick. I couldn't lift my head off the pillow. My husband stayed home with me fetching and carrying for a week. Then he had to go to work. He said to me, 'Babe I have to go to work, I can't take another week off work'. So he went to work.

I remember lying in bed and thinking I can't even go downstairs to make myself a cup of tea. I tried to lift my head off the pillow and couldn't. I opened my mouth and said! '**GOD HELP ME I FEEL SICK!**' Suddenly an Angel appeared over my bed, she was as white snow, in fact whiter than snow, and I don't think there is any colour as white as she was on this earth. Her wings were wide, they were spread out across my bed, I remember looking at the feathers and saying, WOW, WOW, in her hands she was holding a cup. The cup was pure white, not a mug a cup, a china cup. Both her hands were cuddling the cup. She said to me '**DRINK THIS, IT WILL MAKE YOU BETTER**'. I remember trying to lift my head up to drink and couldn't, she gently put her hand under my head and lifted it towards the cup and I drank, then she reversed backwards from me flapping her wings and said to me, you will feel better then she disappeared. I remember lying there thinking how awesome, and then I got up and went downstairs and made myself a cup of tea. Within a day or two the swelling went down, no more headaches and I went back to work that same week. What a God we serve, he said he will never leave us, he said when our mother and father forsake us he will be there. Praise God. The Bible tells us that he will be with us; my experience was a prime example.

> **Deuteronomy 28:1–14; God's promises and blessings to us.**
>
> **Hebrew 11:1; have faith and hope I urge you to look to no one but God. I urge you to look to him who is able I urge you to look to no one but God. I urge you to look to him who is able. Remember, Faith is the substance of things hoped for, you might not see it in the natural straight away but it is there for us to take.**
>
> **2nd Peter 3; proclaims the word of God in your mind. We have access to all things by grace. I say again take heed, eat sleep and drink the words of God always. Profess God's word always, I walk**

down the road talking to God, people look at me to see if I have a ear piece in my ear talking to someone, then they look away. I don't care who looks, God is my source, he is my healer, he is my strength, he is my heart beat, he is my, everything. So let them look. Sometimes my children would asked me, mum who are you talking to? God I said.

CHAPTER 5.

How can we fail with God's Promise.

Please read on.

How can we fail with God's promises to us? We fail because we do not follow his divine instructions. We fail because we are Luke warm, and we fail because we are up today and down tomorrow. We fail because we have no faith; we fail because we focus on our situation and our problems. We are not living and walking in the spirit we are walking in the flesh. The Bible says let everything around us be shadows, what we do not realise is that we are in a better position today compared to the people in the Old Testaments, Hebrews 9:6-11 the high priest offer blood of goats and cows as sacrifices', to God, well that's because those people had no choice but to go to a High Priest and offer up their sacrifices of animals for their sins. The Priest was the only one who could go into the temple and with the sacrifices e.g. a lamb burnt as a Burnt offering offer it up to God and asked for forgiveness on a person's behalf. That Priest was chosen by God and he was sanctified, therefore no other person could enter the tabernacle.

But, today I thank God that he sacrificed his son Jesus. He was the lamb and we are redeemed forever. We are forgiven of our sins, praise God. The devil may knock Us here, he may knock us there. The bible said the righteous will fall, but remember with the blood of Jesus we are redeemed forever, we were purchased with a price. A price that belongs to Jesus forever. He was that lamb that was led to the slaughter. He died so that our sins no matter what it is, has been forgiven. We are now free and we don't have to slaughter a lamb and offer it up as a burnt offering to God for our sins. Think about it, if the Priest used the blood of a calf as a sacrifices', as a burnt offering and rub it on a man that sins to make him free, how much more is the blood of Jesus? This means that we now have direct entry to God. Hallelujah.

We can now speak to God anywhere we are through prayer. No Priest needs to go into the Tabernacle on our behalf. You see when Jesus died on the cross, he conquers all; Colossians 2:14 & 15. Let the peace of Christ rule in your hearts, to which you are called in one body, and be thankful. Yes be thankful come into agreement with God, put on the helmet of Salvation, put on peace **I urge you to look to no one but God. I urge you to look to him who is able**. **I urge you to look to no one but God. I urge you to look to him who is able** very day when you wake up I urge you to put on thankfulness, open your mouth and thank God for lifting up your head, you know you didn't wake yourself up, thank God for your wife or your husband, your children and grand and great grandchildren, your families, friends neabours, and everyone you come into contact with, that day. Set the paste at the begining of the day, speak theing in place and expect it to happened. as my Bishop would say expect the unexpected.. Thank him for a new day, think of the people who didn't make it through the night, being blessed with a new day means restoration. It means you are new every day. A new day, new beginning, God's blessings and favour, tell yourself (I am new every morning), and remember God is compassionate -. This is your opportunity to speak to him and tell him what you want. He knows your heart and if what you are asking for is right for you he will give it.

I need to remind you that God is not just there for us to keep asking for things. As I mentioned previously you must know God for yourself, have a relationship with him. **2nd Chronicles 7: 14** He said if my people who are call by my name will humble themselves and seek my face and turn from their wicked ways, then will I hear from heaven and forgive their sins and heal their land.

Seek his face because if you don't you will just be a carnal fleshy Christian. **Philippians 3:9-11** says Paul wanted a deeper relationship with God. To sum it up, Jesus died for our sins, but what Paul is saying is that to have a deeper relationship with God we have to die for our self. If you don't know what to pray for, ask God to work in you, ask him to change you, ask him to work in your life. Ask him to transform you.

Exodus 17:8-16 God is Jehovah NISSI, he is your banner, he is Jehovah SHALOM, the Lord is my peace, he, is your peace. Be peaceful he said to cast your cares on him, he is your King. **Psalms 25:1** said in you 'O Lord My God, I put my trust! I urge you to get dressed spiritually, put on the clothe of righteousness',

What happens when we speak to God, we declare and create the atmosphere for manifestation to come **Isaiah 46:10** God said 'I am God, and there is no other, there is none like me, declaring the end from the beginning and from ancient time's things not yet done, my counsel shall stand, and I will accomplish all my purpose'. What more do you want? These are God's words. It is so easy, there is nothing complicated about life, all we have to do is to follow him. I say it again life is about having a balance between the spiritual and the flesh. Remember when you are in a situation and you are asking God to get you out of it, God won't get you out of it. He will help to get you through it and get you to a better place to help other people. Therefore ask God to give you favour. It is important to pray for favour. Remember there is power in the word of God. God's word is so power- full that he will come through for you. Remember, in our darkest moment he is there, planning and working on our behalf and he will take us through the darkness and lead us into the light.

CHAPTER 6.

How can you be alone?

1st Corinthians 3:16 'Do you not know that you are the temple of God and that the Spirit of God lives in you?'

1st Corinthians 6:19-20 'Do you not know your body is the temple of the Holy Spirit who is in you, whom you have from God, and you are not your own?'

Remember you are bought at a price, to glorify God in your body, in your spirit and with a true heart. Why? It is because, we belong to God and for that reason we are no longer strangers and foreigners but, we are now fellow citizens with the saints and members of God's family. Having been built on the foundation of the apostles and prophets and on Jesus Christ himself who is the Chief cornerstone, in whom the whole building, being joined together, grows into a holy temple in the Lord and in whom you are also being built together- a habitation of God in the Spirit. **Ephesians 2:19-22**

This leads me on to the 7 principles to activate all the power we have within us to do God's will and to live a peaceful and happy life.

I will be the 1st person to put my hand up to say it took me a long time before I fully understood all these principles and to put them into practice.

1. **Worship:** -

Man must develop and have an understanding of spiritual rebirth by accepting God's free gift of eternal life. The gift of eternal life has been given to us freely. It didn't cost us gold, silver or bronze, it cost us nothing. God gave it to us freely. The only person it cost was God losing his son, and his son Jesus losing his life.

Think about it, do you know anyone who would give up their life for you? I don't know anyone who would give their life up for me and if I am honest I would not give up my life for anyone. But we can't blame anyone for the way we think. It is only because of our mindset on living life in the flesh and not in the spirit. You see we developed materialistic things we have around us. Living, in the flesh, we learnt to accumulate things of the world, we selfishly owned things, we selflessly yearned to have things which mean us no good, and we selfishly worked and gathered things of the world around us. By doing so we forget one of the most important things in our life, something that we were born to do and that is to; worship God. Did you know we were born to worship God?

How about starting right here and now?

We have come a long way off from going into the temple to meet with God; we have come a long way from offering burnt offerings to God for our sins.

John 4:21-24 we will see that worshippers would have to travel to meet with God.

With Jesus dieing for us he gave us the freedom to worship and speak to him twenty four seven, morning noon and night anywhere, any place, any minute of the day or night. 24 hours a day and 52 weeks per year. Think about it, what a privilege we have, what a honour to be able to speak to someone any time we need him. I don't know anyone in my lifetime that I could speak to twenty four seven, Read **Ephesians 2:19-27** and see the freedom you have been given. We must not let things of this world take away our focus of Worship; Worship is a vital tool to develop a relationship with God. It is our single focus; our one objective of worship is God himself.

We must worship God with a true heart. Remember I said this before, God looks into our hearts and not our outer parts, he doesn't want to see false action. What he wants to see is a true heart with the action. Now to worship God you must have knowledge of him. Once you have knowledge of Him you will then develop a relationship with Him by; reading his word- The Bible, trusting him, having faith in him and taking him unto yourself as a father and a best friend. I urge you to keep him as a bosom pall, keep him close to your heart, follow his instructions and remember he is your heart beat, He is God.

2nd Kings18:4 tell us that God dismantles things that are not true around him. He doesn't want anything false so please do not worship with a false heart, please do not worship on the surface, please do not worship with a lie, Do you not fear God? Are you scared, it scares me this is why I try to do what's right at all times?

Remember worship begins with our spirit and not with our emotions. We do not worship God with our feelings or circumstances. True worship take place in spirit and in truth as Jesus emphasises. John 4:24 tells us that the Holy Spirit is the Spirit of truth. Remember, the Holy Spirit lives within us. That alone has given us the perfect tool to worship God in Spirit and in Truth.

John 16:13 Jesus is the Person of Truth and he said, 'the words that I speak to you are Spirit, and they are life'. Worship is a lifestyle John 6:63-66.

> NOTE: I said worship is a Lifestyle meaning how we live our life daily, how we conduct ourselves to our fellow man. Worship is not a religious exercise. It is based on our attitude, how we look after our family, our home, and motives, how we work for our employer and how we conduct our self. This is worship.
>
> John 9:31 says if anyone is a worshiper of God and does his will. He hears from him. Praise God! I leave you with this: worship is everything I am responding to, everything God Is. Amen. Start worshiping God, change your lifestyle, change your attitude, and change your approach to others. Most of all worship with a true heart!

CHAPTER 7.

2. Thanksgiving

As Christians, it is vital that we glorify God and be thankful.

By doing this it leads to salvation.

Wow! Salvation, we are talking serious business now. Salvation, if we don't have salvation we have nothing, we are nothing we merely exist.

Let me repeat this, without salvation we are nothing, we merely exist.

Take heed; be thankful for everything, if you have very little money be thankful. My dear grandmother, God rests her soul, used to say, 'if we look after the pennies, the pounds will look after themselves'.

Be thankful, in the morning, be thankful in the afternoon, be thankful in the evening and at night before you go to sleep, reflect on your day, and think about how grateful you are to God for waking you up in the morning and keeping you through the day. Remember, we have no guarantee that because we wake up in the morning, we will live through the day, therefore reflect on the day and be thankful to God, offer up a prayer of thanksgiving to him.

Be thankful that he keeps you, your family and friends through the day. Remember thankfulness leads to salvation. Some of you might be thinking what is salvation? Salvation means: save, it means rescue, redemption, restoration, it means preservation.

Now let me tell you that the opposite of salvation is destruction. Can you see why you need to be thankful? If being thankful leads to salvation, then why not do it?

Ephesians 6:6 tells us that God's will for us is to be thankful, and this can only be done from the heart, you see when our hearts are drawn to his heart, we are united to him and can therefore fulfil his will.

Having a thankful heart, one would learn to appreciate having fellowship with God and a desire of wanting to draw nearer to him. It should also give you a yearning to be like him, fellowship with God, develop a love affair, and it will give you fulfilment and joy. The thankful heart should lead to giving thanks to his name. It should be the fruit from our lips, and it should be an important part of our life. We should vocalise our thanksgiving in abundance to God and have an attitude of thanks in every situation and circumstances as we go through life.

Thessalonians 5:18 reads: 'in everything give God thanks, for this is the will of God in Christ for you'. Hebrews 13:15 reads: 'Therefore by Him let us continually offer the sacrifice of praise to God, that is, the fruit of our lips, giving **thanks** to his name always'.

2. Thanksgiving

Proverbs 18:20-21 A man's stomach shall be satisfied from the fruit of his mouth, and from the produce of his lips he shall be filled. Death and life are in the power of the tongue, and those who love it will eat its fruit. Wow! I urge you to have a good heart, be truthful to yourself pray with a true and thankful heart.

Remember we are dealing with the heart, without your heart you cannot live, without a heart who are you? God looks into our hearts. Imagine going around with; a damaged heart, full of hate, lies and all sorts. Ask yourself what your outside appearance will look like. Trust me we can hide things internally for a while but It will soon surface, you see, what hidden in the dark will sooner or later comes to light. It will eat you up; it will send you mad, it will create a demon so much so that you yourself will not even recognize you.

I can remember as children in school when someone said something not nice to us, we would reply: 'sticks and stones may break my bones but words will never hurt me'. That's a lie, it's all lies, words can hurt you, it gets rooted so deep inside you that it creates a better root, causing you to develop hate towards that person.

What most of us don't realise is that our tongue is such a dangerous weapon that it can kill us, it can damage you for life, and it can send you mental. I always say to my children; be careful what comes out of your mouth, be careful when speaking about other people. I am always telling them to think before they talk, speak good over others and when doing so, make sure what you are saying is the truth and coming from their heart. **Matthew 15:11** Reads: 'it's not what goes into a person's mouth that defiles you it's what comes out of a person's mouth that defiles a person'. My God! I will say it again, read your bible, follow instructions, if you don't understand what you read ask God to give you understanding and clarification. Be careful what you say, have a true and thankful heart.

CHAPTER 8.

3. Love

Love starts with God. We all know about Adam and Eve; I won't go into it, if you don't know read the book of Genesis. Now God loves us so much that after he created Man, he gave us everything we need with an instruction. But disobedience causes us to be the people we are today. God loves us so much that even after we disobeyed him he still does something beyond our wildest dreams to save us from our sins.

John 3:16 Reads: 'for God so love the world (US) that he gave his only son to die for our sins, that whosoever believes in him shall have ever lasting life'. Wow!

Jesus also teaches us about love, Love one another he said, love your neighbour and love ourselves as God loves us.

When we fall in Love with God there is a complete abandonment of self, therefore we are not concerned with how others see us or how we conduct ourselves. Others may even look at us and our behaviour and call us foolish.

Why, it is because they do not understand what we have found and what we have. Our family and friends see the change in us and in many cases they cut us off totally.

Read **Acts 2:1-47.** I read this quote somewhere in a book and I never forget it. It is reasonable to be foolishly in love with God. Wow!

Matthew 22:35-37 Jesus was asked which is the greatest commandment in the law, He answered, to love God with everything that we are. **Psalm 113:3** tells us that since the sun is always rising and setting, there will always be believers somewhere demonstrating their love for God.

Think about it, what an amazing feeling to be in love, I mean to really fall in love,

When you know, that, this feeling which you are feeling, for an individual is really and truly love. Not Lust but love.

I remember when I found God, I wanted to shout out in the streets and tell everyone, when I was at home I wanted to open the window and shout to the passers by how I found Jesus, I found real Joy, I found Love. My husband, children and family could not understand, why, I would talk and talk and show them scriptures in the Bible. I was so excited; I couldn't wait for Sunday service, and mid week service. Don't get me wrong I prayed and worshiped God in my home also in-between the Church services.

The feeling I felt reminded me of when I fell in love with my husband, can't wait to see him, can't wait to be in his presence, can't wait to talk to him, can't sleep, can't eat. What an emotion time that was.

Many people get confused with love and lust. But if you know God for yourself and have that relationship with him and fall in love with him then you should have no problem choosing a mate that you love and your mate loves you also.

Remember, God's love remains forever. God Love is the Agape Love. Man's love dies and many times we find it is all words and not true, it is not coming from the heart. Or, even if it was true at the time the words were spoken, something happen to make that person to change his or her mind later on, Remember what I said previously, God looks into our hearts but man looks on the outer parts, there is a saying, so true to its word, never judge a book by its cover. God Love stays the same forever, from the beginning to the end.

God never change his mind even when we change, he still love us!

1st Chronicles 16:34 Ezra wrote, 'oh give thanks to the Lord, for he is good and his steadfast love endures for ever'.

Deuteronomy 10:12-22 Reads: 'and now Israel, what does the Lord your God require of you, but fear the Lord your God, to walk in all his ways, to Love him, to serve the Lord your God with all your heart and with all your soul, and keep his commandments and states, which I am commanding you today for your good. Behold, to the Lord your God who has the heaven and the earth in the palm of his hand. He God owns the earth and all that is in it. Yet the Lord set his heart in love on your fathers and chose their offspring after them, you above all peoples as you are this day. Circumcise therefore the foreskin of your heart, and be no longer stubborn, for the Lord your God is God of gods and Lord of lord, the great and mighty, and the awesome God, who is not partial and takes no bribe. He executes justice for the fatherless and the widow, and loves the sojourner, giving him food and clothing. Therefore, for you were sojourners in the land of Egypt. You shall fear the Lord you God. You shall serve him and hold fast to him, and by his name you shall swear. He is your praise. He is your God, who has done for you these great and terrifying things that your eyes have seen. Your father went down to Egypt seventy persons, and now the Lord your God has made you as numerous as the stars of the heaven'.

After reading this it tells me that this instruction was not only for the people who God brought out of Egypt but it is also instructions for us today. It is instructions for me and you. Instructions for us to; keep his commandments love him truly and also to love a foreigner who comes into our country.

Deuteronomy 11:1 -22 tells us to love and serve the Lord always.

I urge you to love the Lord, I urge you to fear the Lord, remember he takes no bribe therefore do not bribe him. And most of all Love him with a true heart and love each other. One of the commandments given by God is to love your Nabors as yourself, in other words, treat your nabour as you would like to be treated, show them love the way you would like them to show you love! Live the good life, the life God wants us to live by showing love to all.

Psalm 115:1 reads: 'Not to us, O Lord, Not to us but to your name be the glory,

Because of your love and faithfulness'.

CHAPTER 9

4. Praise

You need to make praise a lifestyle to enable you to love.

Think about it, when you love someone you compliment them. In a way, you praise them, you adore them. What I am trying to say is, without love there is no praise.

Love comes from the heart and from that love creates a development of praise.

Therefore if you love God you will without a doubt praise him!, you will make praise a part of your life style, you will offer up sacrifices of praise. Love and praise should become one, why you may ask? It is because they both come from the heart. Can you see where I am coming from? Do you understand what I am saying? I hope so. I hope it makes sense. I truly hope you get it.

Ephesians 4:15 read: 'But speaking the truth in love may grow up in all things unto him who is the head-Christ'.

Colossians 3:16 Reads: 'Let the word of Christ dwell in you richly in all wisdom, teaching and admonishing one another in hymns and spiritual songs, singing with grace in your hearts to the Lord'. Now can you see what the Lord requires of us, his instruction to us is to dwell in the word, and he will dwell richly in us with wisdom and by getting wisdom we are to follow the advice given to us? We should use it to instruct or counsel each other in spiritual songs and psalms to Him.

These are instructions given to us, what more do we want? God is there for us; his word washes us so that we can praise him with a clean heart. Remember, God's Word is full of knowledge, and we should administer that knowledge into ourselves. By doing this it should increase our praise.

Praise makes us feel good, praise makes us feel alive, and praise makes us feel wanted and needed by our loved ones, our peers or people we come into contact with. Think about how God feels when his people who know him praise him. Think about it, praise is a part of our life, we all crave it, we all need it sometimes, don't get me wrong, when I said we all need to be praised I don't mean that people should bow down and praise us- No! The only person we should be bowing down to is God. What I mean is that a compliment can be a form of praise, thanking someone can be a form of praise and showing gratitude can also be a form of praise.

Because God loves us so much, He gave his son, so that we do not perish. This alone should give us the desire to return our love by giving ourselves to him, by showing our gratitude through praise and our service to mankind. We should use our

4. Praise

love for him as a foundation for all our praises to eternity. Then when praise becomes a lifestyle, we show we are committed to loving God with all that we are. We are to praise him because his love never fails, praise him and our praise will be permanent.

Praise is an expression of our experience with God, this is why it is important to continue to discover him in his word daily (Read Your Bible) because by doing this, you will without a doubt develop a relationship with Him and you will learn to know Him for yourself.

Remember there is no hope without Jesus, develop a lifestyle of praise.

Chapter 10

5. Warfare

Warfare?, You may ask, yes my friend warfare, I am not talking about war we hear of in the natural and around the universe where man sees it fit to govern, control and want what other have. Or to take control and occupy territory to dictates our lifestyle, where, human lives there is always suffering at the hand of the oppressor. This is clearly control and we live and see it, hear of it everyday of our life. But for those of you who don't know, there is another form of warfare we all have to fight and battle with daily. I am talking about warfare of the spirit.

As followers of Christ we must be prepared to stand against the enemy (Satan) otherwise we will lose the battle, without a doubt I guarantee you that you will be fighting spiritual battles daily.

Let me take you back to the origin of Warfare. When, God created Satan or Lucifer another name he is also known by, and other angelic beings. He anointed Satan with special ministry functions. God's Intentions was for all his created angels and humanity to; love, serve, worship and praise him. But Lucifer gradually took his eyes off God and placed them on himself. His desire became more important than the desire to please God, the God who loved him, created him and anointed him. He became self important and stopped worshiping God. He began to idolise himself, Ezekiel 28:2 tells us how Satan saw himself, he saw himself as perfect, full of wisdom and perfect in Beauty. How he surrounded himself with precious stones, Topaz, Diamond, Onyx, Sapphire, Emerald, and that he were sitting on Gold, and placed himself on the mountain, this is how Satan saw himself as rich, powerful and great.

His imagination got the better of him. He thought he was greater than God (Greed, we are never satisfied) and he started to demand worship which he felt he was worthy of. Therefore he started to place greater worship to himself than on God, because he believed he could replace God. He wanted to have control of every angelic Being in Heaven, to be worshiped as God was. He had some angels who followed and worshiped him. What Satan didn't know was that he was no match for God. He sees himself as Gods equal, but he is no match for God. Why? Some of you may well ask yourself, well, it's because he was created by God therefore his power was limited and because of his sinful nature he was cast out of heaven. By God the One God who created him.

God cast him out of heaven. From that day Sin was born into the world. Read: **Isaiah 14:11-17.**

Thank God for Jesus, on that cross at Calvary where Jesus died and with his death Satan now knows that he has been defeated.

But because of his greed and crave for power and desire to control, he will try to control and deceive men.

I have news for you, remember! Satan was in heaven he knows of all the good things stored up there for us, he will do everything in his power to stop us getting there. He will put temptation in your way, he will go to any length to try and overcome you.

You will know him for who he is; his word do not stand he will change his mind and he comes to you like a thief in the night, you will know him by his character.

This is why it is important to stay focused and make God your centre piece in everything you say or do daily. Keep him close to you, and remember God has now placed him under your feet to stamp on him and fight the good fight, to win the battle and overcome with God on your side. Amen.

CHAPTER 11

6. Restoration and Salvation

Finally after all that is said and done, what is the end result you may ask yourself?

The end result is God's promise of restoration and salvation.

I urge you to remember that God's word stands forever. His word never changes it remains the same yesterday, today and forever. His words remain the same morning, noon and night even in the darkest place his words stands.

Restoration:-

Remember we are new every morning, from the minute our eyes open. God give us a new day, a new beginning a new lease of life. The scripture tells us that we are new every morning.

Yesterday is dead and gone, a new day gives us the opportunity to reflect back on yesterday and see what, where and how we can make a mend and change things we didn't do so well yesterday, how we can make an impact on someone's life, how we can be a better person, how we can praise, worship and be more thankful to God for all he has done. A new day is about how we can have peace of mind, how we can love our family and others, how we can help someone who needs help. A new day is about how we can save a lost soul, we have so much work to do in a new day, but because we take it for granted that we are alive, most of us don't even know why we are on this earth. Most of us don't even know how to be thankful to God for our families and friends, also to be thankful to our families, friends and people around us. Most of us are only thankful when we get a bunch of flowers from our husband or a gift for our birthday etc.

Did you know you can thank your husband other times, I mean times when it is not your birthday? Husbands did you know you can thank your wife for cooking, for washing your clothes? I know many of you take it for granted and think it is her duty. I urge you; husband and wife, sons and daughters, brothers and sisters, aunts, uncles, cousins and friends. Be thankful for each other! Be thankful for them when they are alive. Do not wait until someone dies to think about the goodness they did for you or to see their worth when they were alive. Be thankful for each other, appreciate each other, love each other and while doing so remember, in everything put God first, and do everything with a true heart. That is restoration; RENEWAL OF THE MIND.

7. Salvation:

And after all that, comes, salvation. Praise God. To God be the Glory.

Salvation is for our soul, in the end where will our soul go - Heaven or Hell?

Will our name be in the book of life?

How did we live our life on this earth?

What did we do during our time on this earth?

Did I do what God required of me?

Will my spirit rest in peace?

How will I know I did what was required of me on this earth?

Well we probably won't get everything right but we can try to follow the guidance and principles given to us the Bible.

I know some of you say the Bible was written for people in those days, I have heard many people say that before, but as I say many times before God is the same yesterday, today and forever. His words never changes, His words stand forever. Therefore we can all have salvation if we follow the guidance and principles in the Bible. "Build a relationship with God!"

Remember God gave man knowledge, wisdom and understanding, therefore be prepared to open your heat to receive him and asked God to open your understanding when you read the Bible, by doing that you will find that the knowledge of wisdom will be open up to you. Take these principles and implant them into your life this present day, everything you do, do it with a True heart and watch God work in your life. Watch God come alive in you. Invite him in, surrender to him, let him do the work that needed doing in you and you will see a change in your daily walk with him. Talk with him, laugh with him, cry with him and he will lead you into salvation. Ecclesiastes 12:1-7 Reads: Remember your creator in the days of your youth, before the days of trouble come and the years approach when you will say, "I find no pleasure in them" before the sun and the light and the moon and the stars grow dark, and the clouds return after the rain; when the keepers of the house tremble,

6. Restoration and Salvation

and the strong stoop and those looking through the window grow dim;

When the doors to the street are closed and the sound of others fades; when men rise up at the sound of birds, but their songs grow faint; when men are afraid of heights and of danger in the streets;

Then men goes to his eternal home and dust returns to the ground it came from and the spirit returns to God who gave it and mourners goes about the streets.

Ecclesiastes 12:13-14 now all has been heard; here is the conclusion of the matter:

Fear God and keep his commandments, for this is the whole duty of man. This is the work of man, for those of you who don't know why you are here this is why: to keep God commandments, Praise and worship him and deliver the good news to others.

Verse 14: for God will bring every deed into judgement. Including every hidden thing, whether it is good or evil.

I urge you to look to no one but God. I urge you to look to him who is able.

Look, to him who is able.

Look, to him who is able.
He can do exceedinary things.
More than all we ask or imagine.
According, to his power, and his will.
That is at work within us.
To him, be glorify.
And to him that will provide.
Be, Glorify.
Be glorify, within the Church,
In the Streets and In Our Lives.
Be Glorify,
Be glorify, in Jesus Christ.
Bring everything to him, in prayer.
And in your Praises
Give to Him, your all.
For Ever, And Ever!
AMEN.

Copyright © Donna Williams

Appreciation

Firstly, I would like to - Thank God for his undying love for me, for keeping me and bringing me this far.

❊ ❊ ❊

Thanks - To me childhood friend Deborah Senior-Foster who has stuck with me
Through all my trials and tribulation –Thank you so much Debbie. Love you Girlfriend, My Sister.

❊ ❊ ❊

Thanks - To my Family, for putting up with my mood swing.
My husband –Len.
My Daughters –Vanessa Williams, Sharon & Rebecca Williams
My Sons Jermaine Williams & Shaun Williams
My Grand Children & My Great Grandchildren. I love you Lots.

❊ ❊ ❊

Thanks - To my Brothers and Sisters, Names are too many to mention. I love you guys.

❋ ❋ ❋

Thanks - To My Spiritual Mother – Mommy Norris (Mrs. Norris Logan)
Thank you for your many hours of prayers with me, your guidance and
Your many words of wisdom and the good seeds you have planted in me – I love you and your family with all my heart.
You never stop you never cease praying and making sure I am ok.
I lost my birth mother and God gave me you. How Awesome is he?
Thank You Mommy!

❋ ❋ ❋

Thanks – To my Step Dad Mr. Eustace Stephens you have been a father to me
from the tender age of 15.
You have seen my hurts my sorrows, my highs and my lows and you never once
Complained, you treated me as thou I am your birth child. I love you. Thank You.

❋ ❋ ❋

Appreciation

Thanks – To My dear friend family and Brother Mr. Clive Powell. Thank you for been there and listening to me and picking up the phone when I call. Thank you. I love you.

※ ※ ※

Thanks - To Dr Mark Goodridge, you were my Pastor from my Baptism and for many years after. I believe that your teaching set a lasting foundation in my life.

※ ※ ※

Thanks -To Pastor Marva Scott you had a big impact on my spiritual life with your many prayers for me and my family, the love you have given us and your kindness I thank you and all the family of Rhyma Christian Ministry. Thank
you so much, I love you.

※ ※ ※

Thanks - To my extended Family at Acts Christian Church, Bishop Mark Nicholson, you saw gifts in me and encouraging me to continue writhing.
Thank you for continuing to nurture me and helping me to grow spiritually.
Thanks to all the Pastors, Leaders, the Congregation and Ushers team. Thank you all so much
Love you!
Thanks to My in-laws – Mr. & Mrs. V & J Williams & Family.

✱ ✱ ✱

Thanks To my friends Mrs. C Blackwood & Mrs. Gloria Williams. Thank
You for been there for me. Love You.

✱ ✱ ✱

Thanks to my family, My Aunts, Joy Gohaghan-Walker, Mrs. Barbara Robinson, Mrs. Beverley and Mrs. Jacqueline White. Thank you for been there for me always. My Uncles and Cousins etc too many to mention.
Especially my Cousin Mrs. Shirley McLean Love you.
Thanks to my friends, Juliet Iroegbu, and Cousin, Sandra Harris. Thank you for your friendship.

✱ ✱ ✱

Finally Thanks – To the Late Mr. Purcell Poole My Dad and The Late Mrs. Gloria Stephens My Birth Parents (Mum and Dad I Love and miss you both dearly.

✱ ✱ ✱

Thanks to my Grandparents – The late Mr. & Mrs. Poole. Thank you for my early years and for loving me. Love You.

✱ ✱ ✱

Not forgetting someone who means the world to me, words cannot explained,

Appreciation

Thank you for the principles and standard you put into my life I still apply them daily and implement them into my children's and grandchildren's lives.
My dearest Grand Mother – The late Mrs. Monica Anderson whom I dedicate this book to. Thank you Granny - your princess the name you gave me.

❈ ❈ ❈

Thanks to my long life friend Mr Victor Kinghorne, thank you for your friendship and faithfulness. Love you.

❈ ❈ ❈

Last but not lease Thanks to my dear friend The Late Mrs. Cheryl Powell.
Another close friend from my teenage years I miss and love you dearly.

❈ ❈ ❈

You all had a part to play in my life, you may not know it but you all help me
To be the person I am today. God Bless you all. Love you Donna.

❈ ❈ ❈

Family and Friends if I didn't mention your names, please don't be offended
I still love and thank you.

❋ ❋ ❋

This book was truly a blessing, it encapsulated the understanding of God in a practical sense. The examples were relevant and ones that I could relate to. Through reading this book my faith has increased and it has really shown me the importance of tusting God and looking towards him, because really, it IS ONLY GOD WHO IS ABLE.

I pray that such understanding will not depart form the Writer of this book and God will continue to elevate her in knowledge and wisdom.

I hope all who read are blessed in reading this book, in fact I am confident you will be! For this is truly inspirational and one to refer to always in your wlk with God."

Thank you Andrea! Your friend, Juliet.

> I hope you were blessed by reading this book even when I was writing it, I was blessed. You see, there is no secret what God can do, what he had done for others, he can do for you.

www.ingramcontent.com/pod-product-compliance
Lightning Source LLC
Chambersburg PA
CBHW071026080526
44587CB00015B/2518